Animals
of the
African Grasslands

Written by James Talia
Series Consultant: Linda Hoyt

WorldWise™
Content-based Learning

Contents

The grasslands of Africa

Introduction

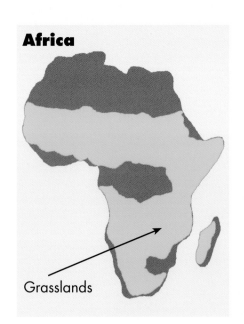

Africa

Grasslands

In Africa, the summers are warm, and most of the rain falls in the cool winters.

Because of this **climate**, grasslands cover large parts of Africa.

Many grasses, bushes and small trees grow in grasslands, but there is not enough rain for tall trees to grow.

Large herds of animals eat the plants that grow on the grasslands, and in turn, predators hunt the animals that eat the plants.

Wildebeest eat plants of the grasslands.

5

Chapter 1
Plant eaters

Great herds of animals travel between the different grasslands of Africa, eating the plants that grow after the rains fall. The grasslands feed millions of animals.

Each type of animal eats different grasses, bushes or trees, and different animals eat different parts of the plants.

Buffalo eat the grasses.

Eland

Springbok

Plant eaters

Monkey

Elephant

Giraffe

Gerenuk

Warthog

Kudu   Wildebeest   Zebra   Rhinoceros   Dik-dik

Grazers

Animals that eat grass are called grazers.

Gazelles eat the new shoots that are close to the ground. Gazelles have long, strong legs, and can travel great distances to find their food.

Warthogs dig in the ground for the roots of grasses. They use their feet, tusks and mouths to dig out the roots from the ground.

A warthog feeds on the roots of grasses.

A herd of wildebeests

A herd of African buffalo

Buffalo also travel in large herds. They eat the tops of tall grasses that grow after heavy rains.

Wildebeests eat grasses and leaves. They live in large herds and must travel long distances to find enough food during the dry season.

Browsers

Large animals that eat the leaves and stems of bushes are called browsers.

Kudu like to eat the **pods** that grow on wattle trees. They **browse** on shrubs and lower branches of trees, and they can hide behind these plants as they eat them.

A kudu

▼ An elephant uses its trunk to feed.

Giraffes eat the top parts of trees.

Giraffes feed on the top parts of trees. They have long legs and necks, and they can reach higher than any other plant eater. They use their thick lips and long tongues to reach around the thorns to eat the leaves of wattle trees.

Elephants feed on trees. They use their trunks to reach the higher leaves and bark of the taller trees.

Chapter 2
Meat eaters

On the grasslands of Africa, meat-eating animals eat plant-eating animals. There are two sorts of meat-eating animals – predators and scavengers.

A predator is an animal that kills its **prey** and eats it. A scavenger is an animal that eats animals that are already dead.

Predators and scavengers hunt for food in different ways.

A lion stalks its prey.

Predators

A leopard creeps towards its prey.

Leopards hunt by hiding in bushes and tall grass. They creep closer to their prey and catch them after a short chase. Then they use their powerful bodies to carry the prey into the trees where other predators cannot reach them.

Cheetahs are fast land animals. If they can get close enough, they can catch most animals.

A cheetah sprints after its prey.

Lions are strong, powerful predators that can bring down large animals such as buffalo or zebras. Their jaws and sharp teeth can bite through large bones.

Lions hunt in a small group called a pride. The pride chases prey towards a lion hiding in the grass. This lion catches it and pulls it to the ground, and the pride shares the kill.

These lions are on the hunt.

A lion catches its prey.

Scavengers

Scavengers feed on sick or dead animals they find on the grasslands.

Vultures and secretary birds are scavengers. They have good eyesight, and as they fly, they look for food. Their powerful beaks can tear food from the body of a dead animal.

Hyenas have the most powerful jaws of all the meat-eating animals. They use their jaws and teeth to crack large animal bones that have been left by predators.

Vultures feed on a dead animal.

A hyena chews on an animal bone.

Chapter 3
Surviving in the grasslands

Living in herds

On the grasslands of Africa, large plant-eating animals live in big groups called herds.

It is much safer for these animals to live and travel in a herd than to be alone. Predators find it difficult to choose which animal to hunt when they see a large group.

Stronger members of the herd **shelter** or hide the younger animals from predators. Sometimes buffalo will **drive** away a lion that tries to attack a member of the herd.

Some animals travel with another type of animal that is taller and can see further, or has a better sense of smell. All types of animals listen and watch for warnings of predators. These warnings can come from animals in their own herd or from other animals.

Watching for predators

Most plant eaters have big eyes on the sides of their heads so that they can see to the front, to the sides and even behind them. They can see over long distances and must always watch for predators.

Plant eaters spend most of their time feeding. They eat and drink by lowering their heads, but when they do this, they cannot see predators. So in a large herd, animals take turns to watch out for danger while others feed and drink.

Zebras take turns to watch out for danger.

Conclusion

Most of the animals of the African grasslands are plant eaters that eat different parts of nearly every kind of plant on the grasslands.

Some of the animals on the grasslands are predators; other grassland animals are scavengers that find and eat the bodies of animals that have died or been killed by predators.

But all grassland animals depend on plants for food.

Glossary

browse to feed on leaves or stems that grow on trees and bushes

climate what the weather is usually like in a place

drive to frighten something and force it to move away

pods seed containers that grow on some types of plants

prey an animal that is caught and eaten by another animal

shelter to protect

Index